Decodable
READER

UNIT 1

Glenview, Illinois   Boston, Massachusetts
Chandler, Arizona   New York, New York

Pearson Education, Inc. 330 Hudson Street, New York, NY 10013

ISBN-13: 978-0-32-898863-1
ISBN-10: 0-32-898863-4

4   19

Unit 1

Week 1
1: I See
Short *a* **1**

2: I Sat
Consonants *Mm /m/ Ss /s/ Tt /t/*........................... **9**

Week 2
3: Mats
Short *i* **17**

4: The Nap
Consonants *Cc /k/ Pp /p/ Nn /n/*........................... **25**

Week 3
5: Tops
Short o **33**

6: It Fit Fan
Consonants *Ff /f/ Bb /b/ Gg /g/* **41**

Week 4
7: A Map
Short e.. **49**

8: We Met Meg
Consonants *Dd /d/ Ll /l/ Hh /h/*........................... **57**

Week 5

9: Fun in the Sun
Short *u* **65**

10: Get Fit!
Consonants *Rr /r/ Ww /w/ Jj /j/ Kk /k/* **73**

Week 6

11: The Quiz
Consonants *Qu, qu /kw/* **81**

12: Vic and Roz
Consonants *Vv /v/ Yy /y/ Zz /z/*.......................... **89**

I See

Written by Betsy McCann

Short *a*

bat

hats

cat

man

hat

High-Frequency Words

a   his   I   is   see

 I see a cat.

 ●

His hat is red.

 I see a bat.

His hat is blue.

I see a man.

 His hat is yellow.

I see hats.

I Sat

Written by Harmony Davidson

Consonant _m_	**Short _a_**
Sam	Sam
	sat

Consonant _s_	
Sam	sat

Consonant _t_

sat

High-Frequency Words

I

I sat.

I sat.

I sat.

I sat.

I sat.

I sat.

Sam sat.

Mats

Written by Dara Lin

Short *i*

his	sit
it	Tim

High-Frequency Words

do	like	one	the	we

17

I am Tim.

I see one mat.

I am Sam.

I see one mat.

Do we like the mat?
We do like it.

See Tim sit.
The mat is his.

See Sam sit.
The mat is his.
We like it!

The Nap

Written by Naomi Kotzmeyer

Consonant c /k/	**Consonant p**		**Short a**
can	nap	tap	can
Consonant m	**Consonant s**		man
man	sat		Nan
Consonant n	**Consonant t**		nap
can	nap	Nat	Nat
man	Nat	sat	tap
Nan		tap	sat

High-Frequency Words

I	see	the

25

I see Nan.

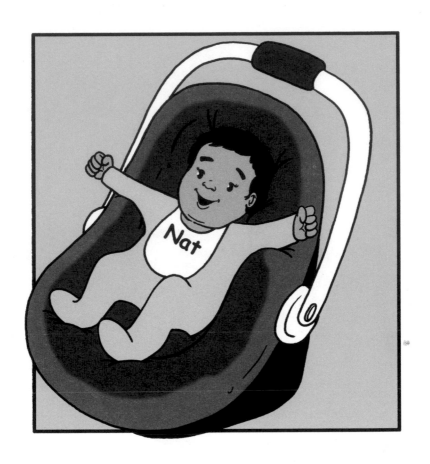

I see Nat.

Nan can nap.

Nat can tap.

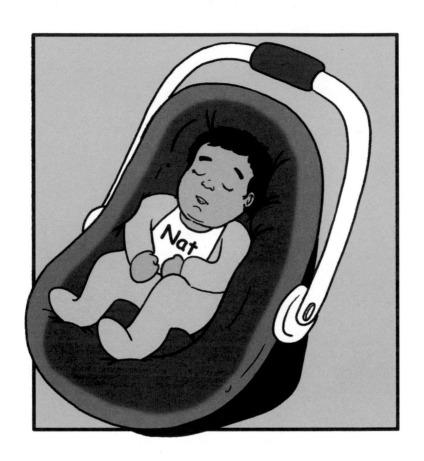

Nat can nap.

Nan can tap.

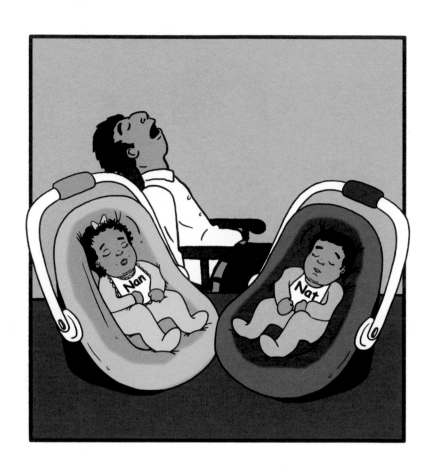

The man sat.
The man can nap.

Tops

Written by Sun Men Chan

Short o

| cot | mop | on | pot | Tom | Tops |

High-Frequency Words

| are | do | is | see | was |
| by | his | look | the | you |

The man on the cot is Tom.

Tops is his cat.
Tops is not on the cot.

Do you see Tops by the can?
Was Tops by the pot?

Do you see Tops by the mop?
Was Tops by the pan?

Look at the map.
Do you see Tops by the map?

Look at the cot!
Tops is on the cot.

We are on the cot.

It Fit Fan

Written by Marguerite Prado

Consonant f				**Short i**
Fan	fat	fit		bib
Consonant b				big
bag	bib	big	bin	bin
Consonant g				fit
bag	big	pig		in
				it
				pig

High-Frequency Words

I	look
like	the

41

Look at the big bin.

Fan sat in it.
Fan fit in it.

Look at the fat bag.

Fan sat in it.
Fan fit in it.

Look at the pig bib.

I like it.

It fit Fan.

A Map

Written by Matthew Pérez

Short e

get	men
gets	net
Meg	pet

High-Frequency Words

by	look	that	they	up
have	see	the	two	

Meg gets a tan bag in a net.

A map is in that bag.

I see men in hats.

They have two pet cats.

They get a look at the map.

The two cats are not by the men.

Look at that!
The two cats are up on the top.

We Met Meg

Written by Desirée Moody

Consonant *d*			**Consonant *j***		**Short *e***		
Deb	fed	Red	Jet		Deb	led	pen
did	led				fed	let	Pep
Consonant *h*			**Consonant *r***		fell	Meg	Red
hen			Red		get	met	well
Consonants *l, ll*			**Consonant *w***		hen	Nell	wet
fell	let	well	wet		Jet	net	
led	Nell		well		**Short *o***		
					got	not	

High-Frequency Words

do	the
see	you

57

Deb let Meg in.

Meg led Pep the pig.

Meg did not see Big Red.
Meg fell in the pen.

Meg fed Nell the red hen.

Do you see Nell?
Get the net, Meg!

Meg met Jet.
Jet got Meg wet.

Meg did well.

Fun in the Sun

Written by Ruby Ivan

Short *u*

bug	hut	pup
cub	mud	sun
fun	nut	tug

High-Frequency Words

as	he	three	to	with

See the hen, the cub, and the pup.
They have fun in the sun.

The three pals have fun with a bug.
The bug is on a nut.

The cub and the pup tug!

The cub is hot.

He and the pup are hot.
They like to sit in the mud.

The hen is not as hot.

The hen naps in a hut.
The three pals have fun.

Get Fit!

Written by Elaine Long

Consonants *l, ll*			Consonant *j*		Short *e*
lot	will		Jen	jog	get
Consonant *r*			jig		Jen
Red	rim	Rob	**Consonant *k***		Ken
Consonant *w*			Ken		Red
Wes	wet	will	Kit		Wes
					wet

High-Frequency Words

a	is	we
do	the	with

73

Rob will jog with Red.
Get fit!

Jen will hop a lot.
Get fit!

Wes will do a jig.
Get fit!

Kit will hit the rim.
Get fit!

Ken is on a mat.
Get fit!

It can get hot.
We will get wet.

We will get fit.

The Quiz

Written by Ming-Kee Lo

Consonant *z*	Consonant *ll*		Short *e*	
quiz	well	will	Bev	well
Consonant *v*	Consonant *y*		pen	yet
Bev	yet			
Consonant *w*	Consonant *qu* /kw/			
well	will	Quin	quit	quiz

High-Frequency Words

a	for
do	the

Quin sat for a quiz.
Bev sat for a quiz.

Quin had a pen.

Bev had a pen.

Can Quin do the quiz?
Can Bev do the quiz?

Quin will not quit yet.
Bev will not quit yet.

Quin can quit.
Bev can quit.

Quin did well on the quiz.
Bev did well on it.

Vic and Roz

Written by Chad Hollis

Consonant _v_			**Consonant _z_**		**Consonant _qu_**	
rev	van	Vic	fuzz	Roz	quit	quiz
			quiz	zip		

Consonant _r_		**Consonants _ff_**	**Short _u_**	
rev	Roz	huff	but	puff

Consonant _y_				
yell	yet	yum	muff	fuzz	sun

		huff	tug
		puff	muff	up

High-Frequency Words

a	is	they	with
have	the	we	

The sun is up.
But it is not hot!

Vic will zip up.
Vic will tug on a hat.

Roz will get a muff with fuzz on it.

Dad will sit.
Dad will sip.
Yum!

"Rev up the van!" they yell.
"We have a quiz!"

Vic will huff.
Roz will puff.
They will not quit.

Will they get the quiz?
Not yet!